Urban Food Insecurity and Coping Mechanisms

A Case Study of Lideta Sub-city in Addis Ababa

Yared Amare

FSS Research Report No. 5

ƒSS

Forum for Social Studies
Addis Ababa

ISBN 978-99944-50-34-3

Forum for Social Studies (FSS)
P.O. Box 25864 code 1000
Addis Ababa, Ethiopia
Email: fss@ethionet.et
Web: www.fssethiopia.org.et

This Report was published with the financial support of the Department for International Development (DfID, UK), the Embassy of Ireland, the Embassy of Denmark, and the Royal Embassy of Norway.

Contents

Acknowledgements

I would first like to thank the Forum for Social Studies for sponsoring this study. I greatly appreciate the logistical support given to the study by Ato Worku Geda, Executive Head of the Lideta sub-city administration and the executive offices of *Kebele* 05/08, *Kebele* 09/10 and *Kebele* 07/14 in Lideta sub-city. I also want to thank W/ro Netsanet Mengistu and Ato Aynalem Mersie of Zema Setoch Lefitih, a local NGO operating in Lideta sub-city, who helped us contact community facilitators for the study. I am grateful for the time and information on policy issues given to me by staff members in the Lideta Sub-city Administration Office - Ato Jemil Teka, Head of the Cooperatives Unit; Ato Bayu Gebre Egziabeher, Head of the Employment and Labour Affairs Administration Core Process; Ato Mesfin Derso, officer in the Health Dept.; and Ato Sisay Tufa, officer in the Small and Micro-Enterprises Unit. I would also like to thank Dessalegn Rahmato for his comments regarding policy initiatives to address urban food insecurity.

I am very appreciative of the excellent work done by Seble Ayalew, who conducted the interviews with me, and the high quality of the data transcription conducted by her, Serawit Omer and Yewilsew Mengiste. I am grateful to Tilahun Hailu, Kebede Bireda and Shimelis Haile Michael, who played an invaluable role in facilitating the participation of the residents of Lideta sub-city who served as respondents in this study. I am indebted to these residents who freely shared their experiences with food insecurity in this very difficult period.

Abstract

In 2009, FSS carried out a qualitative study of the state, causes and impact of household food insecurity, as well as their coping mechanisms, using the case of Lideta Sub-city of Addis Ababa. The study found that food consumption among the poor households that it covered had declined to very low levels over the last several years. The food consumption for an average individual amounted to one piece of bread per individual or even nothing for breakfast, half an *injera* with *shiro* of variable quality or some *qollo* for lunch and the same for dinner.

The causes of the decline in the amount and quality food consumption include rises in the price of food and other basic commodities, losses of jobs or income sources, pre-existing poverty and unemployment, contraction of demand for the goods and services of the poor, and households' decision to invest in the schooling of a family member.

The most immediate outcome of household food shortages is chronic hunger; other impacts include physical weakness, emotional distress, weight loss, illness, and lower educational and work performance.

Households' coping mechanisms include reducing the amount and quality of dietary items, engaging in income generating activities and dependency on several income earners.

The study recommends adopting an urban food security strategy with a safety net programme; improving the grain subsidy programme; strengthening Consumers Cooperatives; promoting employment; expanding commercial and urban food production and processing; and improving child nutrition.

1. Introduction

The food market in Ethiopia has recently been marked by uncharacteristically high prices, a situation that has paralleled conditions in the rest of the world. The causes of escalating food prices in Ethiopia are somewhat specific to it. These include high inflation levels and stagnating food production and supply in relation to increasing demand due to population growth and possibly rising incomes among certain sections of the population. Although high food prices may have raised the incomes of some food producers in the country, they have exacerbated food shortages among food-deficit rural residents as well as urban dwellers that are fully dependent on the market for their food supply. Food insecurity has been extreme especially among the urban poor.

In Addis Ababa, where this study was conducted, surveys have shown that high levels of poverty and food insecurity exist in the city. In 2004/2005, calculations based on the Household Income Consumption and Expenditure Survey (HICES) showed that the proportion of the population in Addis Ababa which fell below the poverty and food poverty line were both around 32% (CSA 2005; MOFED 2008). Given the increases in food prices in recent years and especially in 2008, further rises in food insecurity in the city can be expected.

This study defines food insecurity as a condition in which people lack the food intake they need to lead fully healthy and productive lives. Food insecurity is commonly conceptualized as chronic or transitory. This study focuses on chronic food insecurity which it shows is currently prevalent among the urban poor.

The study aims to provide insight into the state, impact and causes of food insecurity and responses to it among the urban poor in Addis Ababa. It does so through a case study of Lideta sub-city consisting of a detailed qualitative description of current experiences of food insecurity. This includes a portrayal of subjective assessments of the status of and recent trends in dietary adequacy, including dietary amounts, quality and variety. A related concern of the study is the human impact of food insecurity on poor households and their members, including experiences of hunger, malnutrition, ill-health, and low educational and work performance.

The quantitative studies mentioned above indicate that poverty and low incomes are significant causes of food insecurity. This study, which focuses on the perspectives of the urban poor, identifies the multiple, often unexpected and underlying causes of food insecurity.

The occurrence and impact of food insecurity are also influenced by the coping strategies that poor households utilize (Emebet 2008; World Bank 1998). The subject-centered approach in this study affords insight into the diverse strategies that households use to cope with food insecurity as well as constraints on these strategies (Ruel and Garett 2004).

2. The Case Study Site

Lideta sub-city in Addis Ababa, the locus of this case study of urban food insecurity, has some of the poorest neighborhoods in the city. A recent study on urban poverty conducted in three sub-cities with the highest incidence of poverty – Lideta, Arada and Addis Ketema – revealed that Lideta had the highest proportion of households under the relative poverty line for the area, i.e., 53% as compared to 29% in Arada and 47% in Addis Ketema (Netsanet 2008). While Lideta and Addis Ketema both experienced increased rates of poverty in 2008, Lideta was the only sub-city that exhibited generally rising levels of poverty since the mid-nineties.

To represent Lideta sub-city, three *kebeles* – *kebeles* 05/08, 09/10 and 07/14 – were purposively selected. *Kebele* 05/08 is located in the Abinet Hotel area; *Kebele* 09/10 in the Tekle Haimanot area behind the Pepsi factory; and *Kebele* 07/14 is found between the Federal Court and Balcha Hospital. *Kebeles* 05/08 and 09/10 in Lideta sub-city have some of the poorest neighborhoods in the sub-city, characterized by low incomes, very small residential units and unsanitary surroundings. While *Kebele* 05/08 also has a thriving section of medium and small sized businesses, *Kebele* 09/10 has notoriously high rates of poverty, unemployment and crime, its bewildering maze of narrow streets featuring open sewers and overcrowded and poorly constructed housing. In comparison, *Kebele* 07/14 also included a relatively large proportion of middle and even some high income households. In the months since the study took place, however, most of the residences in the *kebele* have been torn down to make way for an urban development project. Residents of *kebele administered* houses have either been allocated similar housing in other parts of the city while those who had private holdings have received new plots of land in replacement and compensation for their houses.

Study participants were selected purposively on the basis of certain criteria, one of which was being in a state of severe poverty. The incomes of selected households ranged from 200 *birr* to 900 *birr* per month and as low as 3-5 *birr* per day. Study participants were also selected from different gender, age and employment categories (See Annex). They included petty traders, daily wage laborers, semi-skilled workers, low-level private and government sector employees, pensioners, the unemployed and beggars, in numbers that roughly corresponded to their demographic importance.

The home visits in which individual interviews were conducted revealed that most respondents lived in housing units of one to two and sometimes three rooms, often small ones. These rooms housed small, medium and large-sized families, which meant that they were often extremely overcrowded. These rooms also commonly served as bedroom/living rooms and bedroom/kitchens. The limited space forced many households to use the roof area for sleeping quarters. The houses were generally made of walls made from wood and mud or corrugated iron. Their condition ranged from those which were well maintained to those which were in various states of disrepair.

Likewise, the houses were furnished at widely differing levels. Some were limited to a bed, a few chairs and maybe a kitchen cabinet, whereas a surprisingly high number of households also had a sofa set, a buffet, a stereo system, a television and DVD player. However, these items were accumulated from extra earnings over the years or remittances from children who were working overseas, while most of the families who owned them were extremely poor and exposed to the severe food insecurity levels.

3. Research Methods

The general methodological approach adopted by this study consists of a qualitative case study of urban food insecurity in Lideta sub-city of Addis Ababa. This approach aims at an in-depth understanding of food insecurity in the sub-city based on a purposively selected sample of *kebeles* and households. Purposive sampling was used to attain a qualitative representation of the diversity of the sub-city in terms of geographic location, poverty status, employment category, gender, age and family size. This meant that although the sample met the needs of a qualitative case study, it is not statistically representative of the sub-city, nor can it adequately represent conditions in Addis Ababa or other urban centers. The study can only aspire to give an indication of the food insecurity situation in other urban areas of the country, hopefully also stimulating quantitative and statistically representative studies on the issue.

The study has utilized qualitative data collection and analysis methods which are best suited to accommodate the subjective and experiential aspects of food insecurity. The qualitative methods that were used were focus group discussions and in-depth interviews. Focus group discussions (FGDs) with male and female household heads were conducted to obtain community perspectives regarding the state, trends in, outcomes and impact of household food insecurity. In-depth interviews (IDIs), again with household heads, were carried out to investigate household-specific experiences with similar dimensions of food insecurity.

Two focus group discussions with nine to ten male and female household heads were conducted with the residents of *Kebeles* 05/08 and 09/10 in the premises of the *kebele* administration offices. Ten household-based in-depth interviews were conducted with 14 male household heads and 16 female household heads in each of the three *kebeles*, for a total of 30 interviews. Given the nature of the subject, quite a few wives and daughters also participated to a lesser or greater extent in some of the interviews with the male household heads.

One local facilitator in each study *kebele* was instructed to select study participants on the basis of the sampling criteria – poverty status, employment categories, gender, age and family size – whom they invited to the focus group discussions and linked with the investigators for the in-depth interviews which were conducted in each of their homes. The investigator for this study conducted the focus group discussions and shared the in-depth interviews with the research assistant. Before the FGDs and IDIs were conducted, interviewers introduced themselves and the objectives of the study to participants, and obtained their consent. The FGDs and IDIs were tape recorded. After the data collection was concluded, the taped interviews were transcribed verbatim by three transcribers. The cassette tape in which one of 30 in-depth interviews was recorded was lost during the transcription process which left 29 IDIs for subsequent analysis.

The transcripts were analyzed manually, by first coding the text under various issues that were of interest in the study. This allowed the statements made by different respondents to be organized according to particular categories of issues. The data in these categories was then synthesized to write up the various sections of the report. Particularly expressive and illuminating statements by respondents have been incorporated into the report as quotes.

4. Study Findings

4.1 The diet of poor households

The diet of poor households in Addis Ababa comprises a limited variety of food items. The most important component of their diet consists of *injera*, the thin flat bread which is made from *teff* and/or other cereals. There are different types of *teff* – white, *sergegna*, black – which have declining levels of desirability and prices. Poor households often use the least costly *teff* varieties and combine them with other cereals which are less expensive than *teff* as a way of maximizing their food supply. *Teff* is combined with cereals such as wheat, maize or sorghum. For instance, 7 kgs of *teff* and 3 kgs of wheat may be bought and milled together, or 4 kgs of teff may be milled with 6 kgs of wheat and 5 kgs of maize to produce the flour that will be used to make the *injera*. A practice that has been widely adopted recently is to use a few kilograms of maize as leaven in a mainly teff-based *injera,* which is seen to yield thicker and more filling *injera* at a lower cost. Alternatively, some households make the flour exclusively from wheat and maize. Although it is desirable to bake the *injera* at home, those who lack the resources to buy even small amounts of grain are often forced to buy *injera* on a daily or per meal basis from other women who bake it for sale.

In poor households, *injera* is usually eaten with *shiro*, a stew which is made from pea flour cooked with oil, onions and if available, *berbere* – processed red pepper. Again, to cut down on costs, a mixture of peas and vetch *(guaya),* or peas, beans and vetch, is often used to make the *shiro* powder. Recorded proportions of these legumes in *shiro* powder were 2 kgs of peas with 2 kgs of vetch, or 3 kgs of peas with 7 kgs of vetch. Apart from the legumes, other ingredients such as oil, onions and especially *berbere* may be either minimal or absent in the *shiro* when households' cash resources are depleted. As a result, the *shiro* becomes less and less tasty.

In addition to the *shiro, injera* may be eaten with lentils or chickpeas stew, or with vegetables such as kale, cabbage, potatoes, tomatoes or carrots. Given the cost of such food items, however, poor households are only able to have them infrequently. Different respondents including a petty trader, guard/carpenter and daily laborer reported that they were able to have lentils or vegetables like potatoes, kale or cabbage only once or twice a week. A manager of a community café, however, said that his family were able to have vegetables only once a month, whereas a vegetable supplier said that they were not able to have vegetables at all because of lack of fuel to cook them with.

Also due to its cost, the use of different types of meat in the stew is commonly as infrequent as the few holidays of the year. Instead, many such households are reduced to a monotonous diet of *injera* and *shiro*. When the latter runs out or as an alternative to it, *injera* is eaten with condiments such as salt, *berbere, mitmita*[1] or a paste made from tomatoes and *berbere* called *sils.*

A common substitute for *injera* is bread in the form of small pieces, *qita,* the flat type, or *ambasha,* the round pie. Such forms of bread are made in the household from wheat flour or by combining wheat and maize. Households which cannot afford to buy the minimal amounts of grain or flour for milling purposes purchase bread on a daily basis. Bread is commonly eaten for breakfast by itself or with tea. In cases where *injera* is absent or unaffordable, poor families may also consume bread for lunch or dinner, with such items as *berbere* or *mitmita*. A daily laborer who headed a family of seven said that his family had *ambasha* with *shiro* or *mitmita* for all meals up to 3 days of the week.

Some of the worse-off households have been using *faffa* - a high energy child food commercially produced for children and donated to poor households – to make *qita, shiro*, or *beso* – a food consisting of the flour of roasted barley. These serve as foods for all household members for at least part of the month as a way of meeting food deficits.

Qocho, which is a type of bread made from the root of the *enset* plant is a staple among households which belong to the Gurage and other southern ethnic groups. It is eaten with kale, *shiro* or *mitmita. Qinche,* which consists of boiled split wheat that is cooked with oil or butter, is usually eaten for breakfast but also as a meal for the elderly at any time of the day. *Qollo* consisting of roasted cereals and pulses is also a common part of the diet. While it is normally eaten as a snack in Ethiopia, *qollo* sometimes replaces at least one of the meals of the day in times of food scarcity. This has recently become increasingly frequent among poor urban households who are facing food shortages.

Food items such as pasta, macaroni and rice, which were consumed fairly frequently in previous years, are now consumed only rarely due to their

---

[1] A hot condiment made from various spices.

increased cost and only in some households. Such households use these foods to break the monotony of the diet especially for children.

4.2 Food consumption levels

Food consumption among the poor households that were covered by the study has declined to very low levels because they can afford to buy only the bare minimum amounts of cereals and other foodstuffs. On average, these households were able to purchase only 10 to 25 kilograms of teff and/or other cereals such as maize per month, the lowest quantities being supplemented by daily purchases of *injera* or bread. They also bought up to 5 kgs of *shiro* to make it last a whole month. Other ingredients are often bought in very small amounts on a daily basis. The wife of a 72 year old tailor who operated a sewing machine at their front gate explained:

> We buy 2 birr worth of edible oil daily which is measured out in bottle tops. We also buy 2 birr worth of onions which only amount to 3 heads of onions. One of them is used for lunch and another one for dinner. We then buy a bottle of kerosene for 2 birr and 2 pieces of coal for another 2 birr. There is no such thing as monthly purchases in our household. *[Family size 6, Kebele 07/14]*

Such small purchases only allow poor families to eat amounts of food that at best are barely enough to prevent absolute hunger. Dietary variety is typically sacrificed to maintain a homogeneous diet that affords access to a minimum amount of calories per day (von Braun et al. 2008). For breakfast, some of the less poor families may succeed in providing one piece of bread or *ambasha* per child or adult to be eaten with tea or just plain water. However, there are many instances in which children and adults may have to share a small piece of bread between two or even three of them. Alternatively, the whole family may share a couple of pieces of *injera* with some *shiro*. In at least half of the study households, adults normatively went without breakfast. Children often went to school without eating anything as well. The wife of the tailor mentioned above, whose family regularly faced severe food shortages, stated:

Every three or four days I may run out of food. So I tell the children there is nothing to eat. They slink away without eating anything. If I have some *injera*, I cut up some pieces, put a few drops of *shiro* on them and give it to them. They may get a quarter of an *injera* each. Today's children, thank God, know everything. They are aware of our condition. They don't bother me much.

Poor urban households of the types that were the subjects of this study typically eat *injera* and *shiro* for lunch if they can. Although it is expected that a person would eat up to one *injera* per meal, almost none of the families appeared to achieve this during the mid-day meal. The largest portion that most of them were able to attain was half an *injera* per person or often a quarter or less. A pensioner spoke of providing two *injeras* for a family of four for lunch, whereas the daughter of a low level *kebele* employee reported that eight family members shared two *injeras* for lunch. A part-time carpenter in his thirties said that his family of five had one and a half *injeras* for lunch. An unemployed older woman who depended on the rental of a room for a living further specified that she had a quarter *injera* for lunch while her daughter had half an *injera,* and a couple of teenage boys had slightly more.

In most cases, the *injera* was eaten with *shiro* which was of variable quality. The lowest quality *shiro* would have no onions or oil, consisting of *shiro* powder and water alone. Some households were not even able to assure themselves a meal of *injera* and *shiro*, and had to be satisfied with some *qollo* and coffee or water. It may also be the case that at least some members of the household would have to miss lunch altogether. A sixty-year old pensioner who headed a family of seven in *kebele* 09/10 said, "If we make some coffee during the day, it will certainly be accompanied with *qollo* as well. If we then drink one or two cups of water, we may forget about eating lunch." A family of ten which was headed by a 50-year old low level employee of the Lideta sub-city administration baked *faffa*, the child food they received as aid, as a *qita* bread that the whole family would eat for lunch on days that the *injera* would run out.

The amount of food that families had for dinner was broadly similar to what they had for lunch. Family members generally shared 2 to 3 *injeras* with some *shiro* among themselves. This meant that they may each get from a quarter to a half *injera*. For instance, a family headed by an older man who worked as a guard and part-time carpenter shared one and half *injeras* with *shiro* among four people. The wife of the man who supplied vegetables to a vendor, on the other hand, stated that their family of more than 10 people shared up to 3 *injeras* among themselves. However, some of the poorest families may have to be satisfied with some *qita* or *qollo* or even miss dinner altogether when they regularly run out of food or cash. While they may try to ensure that at least small children get a quarter or half an *injera,* adults and especially women may go to bed without dinner or only have some *qollo*. A daily laborer in *kebele* 05/08 said that 'there are times that [he, his wife and child] shared one piece of bread. We make some tea, eat *qollo*, drink some water and go to bed.'

Such levels of food consumption are apparently only enough to allow people to barely survive. Respondents were generally extremely dissatisfied with the amounts of food they could eat. They frequently stated that what they had to eat was not enough and that they were not able to eat their fill. A 28 year old married woman who supported a family of six including her parents and siblings by working as a child care-taker and cleaner in a kindergarten run by a local NGO said:

> I know what we eat is not enough. We don't eat enough even when I bake *injera* because I am afraid that I may run out of food before the end of the month. As I am the one who will suffer if it does, I have to regulate what I put on the table so that we do not go completely hungry later on. I cannot just be free with the food. *[Kebele 05/08]*

Number of meals per day

Although the preferred norm in the study communities is to have three meals a day, many households have effectively reduced their food consumption to a maximum of two meals a day. A large proportion of adults go without breakfast, often also as part of the Orthodox Christian fast when people do not break bread until noon or 3 pm. The priority for parents is to provide young children with some breakfast, but many children still go to school without having a meal.

Alternatively, some families choose to have a late morning meal and early dinner as a way of avoiding a third meal. This meal pattern has been labeled the five-eleven or the six-twelve by some to refer to the timing of meals according to the Ethiopian clock[2]. A 40 year old male who was the manager of a community café said, "We have what the university students call 'five-eleven'. It means two meals a day. Breakfast is at five (11 a.m.) as a way of getting close to lunch. At eleven (5 p.m.), there is a meal that serves as both snack and dinner. It is a way of skipping a meal." *[Kebele 09/10]*

There are also a fair number of families in which the adults restrict themselves to one meal a day. They may have adopted this as a regular practice in these days of high food prices or may take it up when their cash and food resources sometimes run out. While struggling to feed children at least two to three times a day, the adults may retain only one meal for themselves on a regular or occasional basis. A 36-year old contract cook who supported a family of four in *Kebele* 09/10 explained how dinner may be optional:

> We don't eat much in the morning. Only my small child eats breakfast [bread with tea). My mother spends the day at church and returns at 4 p.m. to eat lunch. She then goes to sleep. She doesn't eat dinner.... I eat two to three rolls of *injera* with *shiro* for lunch.... In the evening, we make coffee and may eat *qollo* but we may not have dinner. If somebody says she is hungry, we will have dinner. Otherwise, nobody asks to have dinner frequently.

In some cases, even children may have to go on one meal a day. For instance, the 72-year old tailor pointed out that his children had to skip breakfast and only have a minimal dinner up to two times a week. The daughter of a 50-year old man who worked as a low level employee in the sub-city to support a family of 10 people said that his children may have to do without breakfast:

> For instance, we may run out of *injera*. When the children come home from school, they will look for food and will simply leave the house [if

---

[2] The Ethiopian clock starts at the beginning of the day (7 a.m.) and counts up to twelve (6 p.m.) and then continues all over again in the night time hours.

they can't find any]. If I have a bit of money I will give it to them. Otherwise they will just leave the house. This occurs at least two times a week. *[Kebele 05/08]*

Thus, the meal pattern of many families varied from one to two times a day depending on the availability of resources. Indeed, many families were not able to entertain a regular meal schedule due to fluctuating incomes and food stocks. Rather, they altered the number of meals they had from two to three times or one to two times a day according to the food stocks available to them.

4.3 Intra-household differences in food consumption

International studies have shown that even under conditions of food scarcity, there are important intra-household differences in food consumption on the basis of age and gender. In the study area, the tendency is to avoid differences in food allocation among family members apart from the special consideration given to children. A good number of respondents said that family members ate the same types and amount of food, often from the same plate. This is especially the case among the poorest families where the food that could be offered is too small to be divided up among family members. It can also be an important means of reinforcing family solidarity in the face of scarcity.

Significantly, however, families strive to protect young children from household food shortages by maintaining their food intake at an adequate level. A 78-year old pensioner who headed an extremely food-insecure family of seven people justified this by saying:

> We don't give them anything different – where can we get it from? But we [adults] at least cut back from what we eat to give them more. We believe that their stomach and ours are different, that they are not able to tolerate [hunger]. We want them to grow and become somebody some day. *[Kebele 07/14]*.

Some of the ways of protecting young children from food shortages include excluding them from foregoing meals as older children and adults often do when food supplies are limited. For instance, young children are given at least some bread with tea if possible for breakfast while it is quite common for older individuals to skip this meal. Secondly, while adults cut back on their intake at each meal before they had their fill, children may not have to do so. Young children in some households are also given food separately. Special foods such as pasta may be prepared for them as well.

The severity of food shortages, however, can prevent families from giving special treatment to children. Children may therefore be forced to go to school without eating breakfast and even have to miss lunch as well sometimes. Frequently, reductions in their food consumption may only involve elimination of snacks during the day, sometimes on the initiation of children as young as five who are well aware of the shortages their families are facing.

Apart from young children's food intake, the dietary levels maintained by women in poor households is more likely to deviate from other family members, but in the opposite direction. This is because they often cut back on their food consumption in favor of their children and other members of their family (Maxwel et al. 2000). Older women in particular have been observed to reduce their food intake to one meal a day with the justification that their appetites are lower and that it is more worthwhile to favor the young with respect to food.

4.4 Trends in food consumption over time

What is most notable about recent trends in food consumption among poor households is the decline in food amounts and quality over the last several years. According to respondents, this is associated with the continuous rise in food prices and other basic commodities over this period. Noticeable but limited increments in food prices reportedly started four years ago in 2005. However, the sorts of price increases that led to significant cuts in what were already low or moderate levels of food consumption occurred since 2006. Different households date the timing of reductions in their food consumption either to 2006 or 2007, although there were no noticeable differences in their capacities to withstand food shocks.

By far the most drastic hikes in food prices and related rise in food insecurity were said to have occurred in February 2008. The period since that time has been marked by the most severe levels of hardship, according to the testimonies of study subjects.

For some, the impact of rising prices has been balanced by improvements in income due to new jobs acquired by family members. In such households, food security may have improved or remained stable over this period. For a few of the poorest households who make a living from such activities as begging, food consumption a few years ago was just as low as it is presently.

One of the most important outcomes of food price rises in the period since 2006 was the reduction in cereal purchases, especially that of *teff*, by households. At different points in time, households which used to buy 40 to 50 kg of *teff* a month spoke of reducing their purchases to 25 kg and those which bought 25 kgs of *teff* said that they reduced it to 10 to 15 kgs or less. Some household dealt with the high price of *teff* by mixing some of it with wheat and maize for the purpose of making *injera*.

Such cuts in cereal purchases, in turn, led to reductions in levels of consumption of *injera* per meal or per day as households attempted to make the limited supplies of cereals last as long as possible. Others replaced the *injera* with wheat bread to some extent. The wife of the small time tailor mentioned above described the reductions in *injera* consumption they had to undertake in the following way:

> [Before 2008], I used to eat till I was full. I would take one *injera* for myself, eat as much as I wanted and return a quarter of it. Everyone ate as much. Now, we eat about half an *injera* each. It's neither death nor survival. *[Kebele 07/14]*

Similar increases in the price of pulses also led to substantial cuts in their purchase or that of *shiro* flour, which meant that *shiro* which is an indispensable supplement to *injera* had to be reduced from the diet along with the latter. A young daily laborer who headed a family of three described the cutbacks they undertook with the price increments in 2008.

14

> We now share one *injera* between the two of us, whereas we had one and a half to two *injeras* last year. We used to put a proper amount of *shiro* on the *injera*. But with the rise in the cost of living now, we had to bring it down to one ladle of *shiro*. We have to save for dinner some of what is cooked for lunch. It has become a time of difficulty and struggle. *[Kebele 05/08]*

The smaller stocks of cereals and pulses available to households also led to the increasing need to skip a meal or two during the day. While households were more likely to have three meals and possibly an additional snack on any given day in previous days, many have now come to do without breakfast most commonly, and sometimes skip lunch or dinner in addition as well. In a focus group discussion conducted in *kebele* 09/10, a 51-year old pensioner and guard who headed a family of six explained:

> We used to eat 4 times a day. Our children used to have at least a snack of *qollo* or *shiro*. With a little rise in the cost of living, we cut out these snacks. With a further increase in prices, we eliminated breakfast. Now, nobody eats breakfast or a full *injera* for lunch or dinner.

A young girl who lived with her blind grandmother and her own child – both adults begging for a living – compared their meal pattern previous to price rises with the current one in the following manner.

> We usually eat twice a day, breakfast and dinner. If we have breakfast, we sometimes leave out lunch. Sometimes, we may have lunch, too. There are times my grandmother does not eat dinner. [Before the price rises last year], we used to eat three times a day. We had dinner, breakfast, lunch as well as snacks. Now, let alone snacks, we are lucky if we eat our fill for lunch. *[Kebele 05/08]*

The rise of cereal prices as well as that of pulses, vegetables and fruits had another significant nutritional outcome. This was the substantial decline in dietary variety and quality because individual food items were less or no longer affordable and because of the overall drain on household incomes brought about by general food inflation. Respondents reported that they gradually phased out or reduced their consumption of pulses such as lentils and vegetables that are commonly eaten with *injera*. The

60-year old pensioner who heads a family of seven described the reductions in dietary variety as follows: "[Two years ago], we used to regularly vary our diet. For instance, if we eat cabbage today, we won't have it tomorrow. Similarly, we alternated chickpeas, potatoes and other foods. Now, we eat *shiro* everyday of the week". *[Kebele 07/14]*

Similarly, households generally cut down on their purchase and consumption of food items such as pasta, macaroni, rice, meat, milk, eggs and butter. These foods are now consumed either rarely or not at all. Their efforts to cut down on these relatively high cost items and to maximize access to calories meant that they were now restricted to a monotonous diet of *injera* and *shiro* which may or may not be interspersed by the aforementioned dietary items. The man who managed a community café for a salary of 400 birr a month said "It was good previously. We used to put butter in the *shiro.* We would eat meat as well. We had a variety of foods every three or four days. Now, we eat only one thing [*injera* and *shiro*]". *[Kebele 09/10].* Regarding the monotony of their current diet in comparison to the time before 2008, the tailor's wife also said: "We used to have lentils and vegetables like potatoes, chard, and cabbage regularly. At present, to tell you the truth, it is *shiro* and *shiro* [everyday]. Even I get sick of it. However, when my children complain, I tell them to be quiet, to be thankful. My only goal is that even this doesn't run out". [*Kebele* 07/14]

Cutbacks also affected food ingredients such as onions, oil and *berbere* (hot pepper) which made such a monotonous diet of *injera* and *shiro* even less palatable. These ingredients and items such as charcoal and kerosene, which were previously bought in larger quantities, are now increasingly bought in tiny quantities from *chercharo* sales – retail sales conducted by petty traders. This has represented a significant shift in consumers' interactions with the market.

Although families go to great lengths to protect young children from such reductions in the household diet, their dietary intake has also been affected over this time period. More commonly, foods previously bought for children in particular such as eggs, milk and pasta have generally been eliminated from the regular diet. Many households are also no longer giving snacks to children in-between meals like they used to. In some households, children are now doing without breakfast, while older children may miss out on lunch as well on those days when households happen to be particularly short of food. In a focus group discussion held in *kebele* 05/08, a 52 year old male household head said, "Before 2006/2007, most people used to have breakfast. Since then, families have started to eliminate breakfast. Conflicts with children began to rise. They would say 'give me breakfast'. And mothers would say 'where shall I bring it from?'".

4.5 Perceived causes of household food insecurity

Various causes of food insecurity were articulated by respondents in the study. These causes operated in a context of widespread urban poverty associated with very low incomes and unemployment or irregular employment. The failure of people to gain employment arose from insufficient availability of jobs and demand for their products and services, lack of skills and inability to work due to old age or illness. Large family size put and kept some households in poverty.

The most acutely felt cause of food shortages in many of the households included in the study was the significant rise in the price of food and other commodities in recent years (described above). The most drastic price increases occurred over a relatively short period of time, i.e., the last year or two. Such increments forced most of the households to substantially reduce their purchase of cereals, pulses, vegetables, processed foods such as pasta and animal products. The cut backs led to severe food shortages and low levels and quality of food consumption. The very articulate wife of the tailor mentioned above described the role of high market prices as follows:

> It is the increase in the cost of living that brought about food shortages. Otherwise, we would have lived according to our capacity, even if our income is low. Now, our income and the market have diverged. For my daily bread, if I wash clothes for three or four families to get 150 birr, what will I be left with? That is the problem, where is the benefit? It is only a waste of energy. *[Kebele 07/14]*

Respondents had various theories regarding the causes for the steady and at times drastic increases in food prices. It appeared to be commonly accepted that the free market was responsible for the price hikes which contrasted with the regime of price regulation during the previous government. The lack of regulation on grain trade presently is perceived to have given the grain merchants' free reign to raise prices as they see fit. Some also believed that farmers were holding on to the grain they produced because of the better bargaining position vis-à-vis the market they now enjoyed. This position is thought to have emerged from the credit they now have access to in order to engage in such income generating activities as animal fattening. Traders were also said to purchase directly from farmers, buying the crops while they were still in the field and hoarding the grain until prices were higher.

On the other hand, a number of study participants believed that grain is being exported to overseas markets thereby raising local prices. A few thought that it was population growth in relation to limited supplies of grain that has led to higher grain prices.

Grain price rises acted in concert with other factors to bring about or worsen the food insecurity they were experiencing, according to many of the respondents. For some of them, escalating food prices coincided with the loss of a job or income generating activity. A few of the study households which were experiencing food shortages had abandoned income sources such as baking *injera* or weaving cotton due to an illness or physical incapacity. This had obviously diminished their ability to cope with high food prices. Similarly, the elimination of an income source due to the death of a husband or the migration of a daughter to the Middle East resulted in the same outcome for a couple of households. Two older men who were supporting their families on small pensions began to experience severe food shortages when food prices began to escalate.

The closure of a business or employing agency due to the actions of authorities sometimes led to the loss of jobs and consequent food insecurity as well. This occurred in the case of one of the women mentioned above who was a member of a cooperative engaged in baking *injera* for sale, which was subsequently closed due to a road construction project.; a martial arts instructor who became an assistant carpenter after losing a training hall when the *kebele* administration reallocated it for a different purpose; and the manager of a community café who had to close the café due to a high lease payment.

As indicated above, pre-existing low income levels and unemployment in combination with high food prices were also pointed out as the causes of food shortage by quite a few respondents. The former apparently weakened the ability of people to cope with the latter. Notably, a couple of people explained that it was people who did not have a regular salary from a government job or from the private sector that were more likely to be food insecure. We have observed in this study, however, that even those who belong to this sector often face severe food shortages.

The contraction of demand for people's goods and services was also indicated as an important factor behind diminishing incomes and food supplies. Such demand contractions occurred under the inflationary pressures placed on overall incomes. Demonstrating the adverse impact of this on her cloth washing activities, the tailor's wife said, "There is no one who hires [a person to wash clothes]. With the rise in the cost of living, the person who used to hire someone does it himself because he would rather keep the money that he would have paid to someone else".

Some households decide to invest relatively substantial amounts of money on the schooling of a family member in the hope of improving their income in the future. This can impose a huge burden on the household's income and food resources in the meantime. A case in point was the manager of a community café who was paying for his daughter's training in hairdressing under conditions of very low income and severe hardship. The same was true of the young *kebele* employee who was spending 170 birr monthly on legal training despite additional expenditures on previously incurred medical expenses, which left him with only 200 birr to meet the subsistence needs of the 8-person family he was supporting.

Thus, although the high rate of food inflation as an important cause of food insecurity is widely acknowledged among respondents, a larger proportion of them also mentioned additional factors exacerbating its impact or inhibiting their capacity to cope with it. A number of respondents mentioned three or four factors which combined to diminish their food security. An example is the young contract cook who mentioned the termination of her weaving activities due to an eye problem, contraction in the demand for her services, the departure of her daughter for work in the Middle East and the rise in food prices which combined to bring about the food shortages they were facing. Similarly, a 19-year old woman who worked for a small cosmetics firm blamed high rental cost and her husband's irregular employment in addition to food inflation.

4.6 The perceived impact of government policies/actions

Respondents saw both opportunities and threats in government policies and actions with respect to household food security. The sale of subsidized wheat to urban residents that the government embarked upon in 2008 is generally perceived to have had a positive impact on food security. The subsidized wheat appeared to be the only thing that mitigated the impact of high market prices for many households who mixed it with *teff* to make *injera* or used it to bake bread. Nevertheless, some found the minimum quotas of 100 kg too costly and wished that they were able to buy smaller amounts. The prices for which the wheat was being sold currently as compared to previous sales were also too high for many households.

Consumers' associations, which were expected to provide households with grain and other food items at affordable prices, are another component of the government strategy to reduce food security. Most respondents disapproved of these associations, however, asserting that the prices they offered were not much lower than market prices. The reason given for their inefficacy was that they lacked adequate capacity. By comparison, government efforts to control grain prices which were attempted over the previous year were seen as helpful. As shown above, however, many thought such efforts were inadequate as food prices still remained high.

While government loan schemes for various income earning activities could be useful, the lack of space for such activities, the need for a guarantor and a residence, as well as fears of being unable to repay limited the access to and utilization of these schemes. Youth associations designed to create work opportunities for groups of youth were said to be undermined by too many requirements as well as biases against the youth. A young man who was the son of the vegetable supplier explained:

> When we try to get organized, why do they create obstacles by saying 'Do you have a certificate? Do you have work experience? Did you graduate with a degree or diploma?' Ok, so what will happen to us? When things get worse, we are forced to go into crime. So then, they say 'Kereyu (one of the poorest neighborhoods) boys are criminals. Kereyu boys are this and that'. This is because no one gives us any attention. *[Kebele 09/10]*

In contrast, a women's cooperative which run a café that offers affordable meals to poor residents after receiving credit and space from the local administration was an example of a successful initiative. Improvements in salaries and pensions that were aimed at mitigating the effects of inflation were also appreciated by beneficiaries.

While such initiatives were seen to have positive effects on household food security at least in theory, there were government policies or actions that were found to be generally detrimental. As shown above, the free market system was commonly seen as the root cause of the food inflation and food insecurity that they were confronted with. The harassment of poor women and men who engaged in petty trading and other income earning activities on the streets severely weakened their efforts to secure food for their families. The failure to support cooperatives or enterprises which have been closed due to the diversion of the space they utilize for road building or other uses has also resulted in the same outcome.

4.7 The impact of food insecurity on poor households

The high levels of food insecurity that were described above are likely to have major adverse impacts on urban households. This section describes some of the consequences of food insecurity as perceived and expressed by households included in this study. The outcomes discussed are hunger, nutritional or physical status, health and educational or work performance.

Hunger

The most immediate outcome of household food shortages is the chronic state of hunger that adults and children experienced. Many respondents acknowledged that they and their children often felt hungry during days in which they had to miss meals or had to spend the day with only a piece of bread. A 24-year old housewife married to an employee of a private shoe factory talked about the effect on her children when she could not give them a meal.

> We do feel hungry. But if I don't have anything I don't have any alternative but to tell the children so. They would cry and then keep quiet. Since I don't have an option, I leave them to cope with it. Although I feel hungry as well, I tolerate it. *[Kebele 05/08]*

Children were often said to be irritable and cross when they had to be denied lunch or somehow received insufficient food. A 50-year old housewife of a vegetable supplier, whose family members numbered 13, spoke of how the children responded to the inadequate meals she was able to give them.

> If you were to stay till noon, you would see how the children behave. They say 'I am not full. Emaye, I am still hungry.' I have to sit outside when they eat. They come out and say they have not had enough. If I had food, I would have given it to them abundantly. What can I give them if I don't have it? *[Kebele 09/10]*

There were times when the monotony of the diet itself deterred children from eating as much as they would like. Regarding this, the tailor's wife said:

> My children are expected to grow, be educated and do much for their country. But now, they are demoralized by the pangs of hunger because they cannot eat what they want. Day after day they have to eat *shiro*.

And it is not real *shiro* with oil and onions. There are times in which we have to make *shiro* without onions. So they are usually sick of what they eat. So there is hunger in my house. There definitely is hunger. But where can we go? Only God can help us. *[Kebele 07/14]*

Even adults found it difficult to bear when food shortages were so bad that they were expected to skip two meals in a row. The 50-year old employee of the sub-city administration who headed a family of 10, including children and grandchildren, talked about how he reacted when he was denied lunch even after skipping breakfast: "When I come back from work we often have a fight. I say 'how come you don't give me anything after I have spent the whole day at work?' And they respond, 'Did you give us any money [to buy food items] when you left?' I would then not say anything and ..." *[Kebele 05/08]*

Quite a few respondents, on the other hand, talked of how their family, including their children, accepted and tolerated the hunger they felt on a continual basis. This appeared to be a form of adaptation to food shortages. Children would therefore often leave for school without breakfast and not complain because they have become used to it or they are aware of their household's status with respect to food. Children who grew up under deprived conditions were particularly tolerant of hunger. The young man who was an employee of the *kebele* administration described how his family, long accustomed to food insecurity, dealt with days in which food was especially insufficient.

When we leave the house in the morning, the children take what is given to them and thank their mother. Even if they are hungry, they suppress it. They are bound to be hungry. When you tell someone to spend the whole day on one *ambasha*, you can guess what it is like. Even if they are distracted by playing for much of the day as the children they are, they would feel the hunger. But they control it out of shame. It only becomes noisy when we get together for lunch and dinner. Everything is forgotten and it becomes nice. *[Kebele 09/10]*

There were even people who said that they were not hungry despite conditions of overall food insecurity. They claimed that what they ate was enough to satiate them. Others said that they did not feel hungry despite eating insufficient amounts of food. This was partly because they were used to lack of adequate food, some of them not thinking about it while at work.

Regardless of how accepting people are of hunger or food insufficiency, it was known to impair their strength and physical function. A number of respondents said that they often felt weak because of an inadequate diet. In a focus group discussion held in *Kebele* 05/08, a 58-year old male pensioner said, "I am not able to stand for long. If I stand for five minutes, I will fall. I have to either sit or walk. I feel pain even when I am sitting. It is therefore hunger that brings illness. It is because we are not getting a balanced diet". A 54-year old male daily laborer also said:

> I am now losing 'resistance' to tell you the truth. I am even finding it difficult to walk up these stairs to the house. That is because of the food situation. I will start shaking if I lift something heavy. That is because my body is not getting what it needs. We have reached this point. *[Kebele 09/10]*

The study also documented the psychological consequences of sustained food shortages. Respondents talked about the deep emotional distress they continually experienced due to the state or fear of food shortages in their household. Asked how food shortages were affecting him and his family, the young part-time carpenter who heads a family of five in *Kebele* 07/14 lamented:

> It is something that does not hit you physically or shoot at you. But there is a big 'fight' going on within us heads of households. The former would have been better because you would only be wounded or die. It would be a fist or a kick. But [the hunger] is [pressuring] you daily. Plus, it makes you anxious. Finally, it takes you down. Also, the children may be happy today when we buy or cook them something today. But they may not be happy tomorrow depending on conditions. So, it is a 'fight'. That's it!

In a focus group discussion held in *kebele* 05/08, additional psycho-social effects of hunger were expressed by a 52-year old security guard in the following manner, "Hunger is difficult. A hungry person cannot go to sleep. It is a big problem. Hunger denies you peace, denies you love…it denies you peaceful relations with your neighbors, makes you irritable. Hunger by itself is a big illness."

The extended strain of food insufficiency on individuals also appears to have led some of them into a state of demoralization and hopelessness. The daily laborer mentioned above said:

> If I don't get something after I work and there is inflation on top of that, I remain poor, don't I? Actually, I am like a dead person. Can I be called a person? I am living a worthless life. If I did not believe that God should take what he created, I would be happy to destroy myself rather than watch these children [go hungry]. This is the stage I have reached. How can I talk of citizenship, being an Ethiopian, living a life like this?

Physical or nutritional status

Such levels of food shortage can be expected to result in reduced physical or nutritional status among poor urban dwellers. However, a substantial proportion of respondents did not perceive any weight loss in themselves or in members of their family. Some of them may of course have failed to perceive the occurrence of such weight loss. An even larger proportion of respondents, on the other hand, believed that children and/or adults in their family had experienced weight loss or become thinner as a result of food shortages. Regarding failure to gain weight in her children, the 19-year old factory worker said:

> When I take my children to the hospital, the health workers cry out 'why don't you feed the children, don't you have any food, just look at her'. They raise her hands and chastise me if they are thin and bloodless, saying 'you are only breastfeeding her without giving her any other food'. When they get sick now, I make them take holy water or the Holy Eucharist and they get well. I am too embarrassed to take them to the hospital because their weight is so low. *[Kebele 07/14]*

Quiet a few of the adult respondents had also experienced perceptible weight loss. A couple of men stated that they had lost as much as 10 kilo grams in the last year. In addition to inadequate food consumption, a number of respondents believed that their loss of weight was due to anxiety over their food insecurity. The young daily laborer who headed a family of three in *kebele* 05/08 said:

> I have lost much weight in the past year. That's because of anxiety over my child. I worry a lot and that weakens you inside. It is not because of food shortage but because of worrying over my fate. When I am able to work, I can rest in peace at night. On days I have not worked, that's it!

Health

Malnutrition arising from extended exposure to food shortage can also lead to ill-health, although the latter can be caused by other factors as well. A large portion of the respondents stated that their families were healthy despite the food shortages they were facing. Others pointed out a number of illnesses that had afflicted members of their family that they attributed to food insufficiency. Some respondents said that their children were frequently sick from a cold, cough or sore throat ever since their family started to experience food insecurity. In a focus group discussion held in *Kebele* 09/10, a 35-year old physically disabled man who worked in a *kebele* café said:

> Children today are not gaining weight, they are losing it. Therefore, they cannot resist disease. Now, even when they catch a cold, they stay in bed. Recently, my son got sick and I took him to the clinic. They asked me why I did not feed him balanced food. I cannot even feed him once a day, and only one type of food. The doctor said that he was sick due to malnutrition. Thus, the children are frequently sick. We are also often sick. *[Kebele 09/10]*

A few respondents also indicated that a child of theirs has been having anemia or dizziness from lack of adequate nutrition. Adults as well were said to be vulnerable to colds and headaches. Several respondents reported that someone in their family had fallen victim to stomach illnesses that they said were caused by insufficient or undesirable foods, as well as anxiety over food insecurity. For instance, the manager of the community café talked about the illnesses such as kidney and stomach conditions and high blood pressure that he and his wife had developed due to anxiety over meeting their family's food and other needs. Finally, a couple of respondents mentioned local illnesses like *berd* and *mitch*, conditions thought to arise from exposure to environmental elements such as cold air and the sun to which people were made vulnerable by food insufficiency.

Educational and work performance

Lack of adequate food can adversely affect children's educational attainments and adults' work performance. Again, responses from study participants regarding this issue were mixed. A good fraction of them stated that neither types of performance were affected by inadequate food consumption. In contrast, some respondents reported that children in their households or in their community failed to go to school either because they were too hungry or because they had to work in order to contribute to the household food supply.

Others were not able to study after school also because they had to work. Some children were said to find it difficult to follow lessons or study adequately when they had not had enough to eat. A teenage daughter of the man who was an employee of the sub-city administration said, 'If you are hungry when at school, you are likely to be thinking of something else. You don't concentrate on the lessons as much' [*Kebele* 05/08].

Some adults also found that their capacity to work effectively was compromised when they had not eaten adequately. This was especially the case among those who were engaged in physically demanding work such as cloth washing, daily labor and food preparation. For instance, the young daily laborer for the telecom sector said:

> If I have not had breakfast, there are times I would have to stop working. I become sick in the stomach. I can't bend and straighten up. My stomach would be 'grinding' on its own, which hurts me. Then I would have to stop working, which means I don't get paid. When I stay away from work for too long, another person will be hired in my place. [*Kebele* 05/08]

The other daily laborer interviewed in the study also said that his hands and legs would shake when he lifted heavy objects at work. Similarly, the wife of the tailor mentioned above who also washed clothes for her income described the impact of hunger on her capacity to work as follows:

> Now, I can't work if I want to because I know the state of my stomach. My body would start to shake. I can't keep my balance. If I carry two containers of water, I would have to sit down. I can't do it. I will start shaking. But it would not prevent me from working. I would have to rest a lot while working. I would wash half of the clothes and save the other half for the next day. It is very difficult. An illness is better than such want and hardship because it can be cured with medical care. *[Kebele 07/14]*

4.8 Coping with food insecurity

In addition to the various causes of food insecurity described above, households' coping mechanisms are important determinants of their vulnerability to it. Such coping mechanisms fall into such categories as the regulation of food purchases and food consumption, income earning activities, asset sales, social mechanisms such as loans and other forms of social support, and dependence on aid. These coping mechanisms take particular local attributes that are described below.

Food purchases

As households are faced with rises in food prices and/or shortfalls in resources, one of the initial and significant steps they take are reductions in the levels of food and other items that they normally acquire from the market. In the study communities, households reduced even the normally small amounts of food that they purchased in a significant and unprecedented manner. At various times in the last few years, but especially in the past year and a half, households cut back the amount of *teff* they purchased on a regular basis. Different households reduced their *teff* purchases from 70 to 50 kgs, 50 to 30 kgs, 25 to 10 kgs, etc.

In addition to absolute reductions in the purchase of cereals, these changes could be in the form of a shift towards buying cheaper types of *teff* and other types of cereals such as wheat and maize. The latter could be mixed with *teff* in order to bake less preferred types of *injera*.

The availability of subsidized wheat in the past year has allowed households to replace part of the *teff* they normally purchase with wheat. Because the minimum amount of subsidized wheat that can be purchased by one household, i.e., 100 kgs, and its gradually growing price over subsequent months made the full use of this source impossible for many poor households, they resort to buying a single households' allotment in groups. Alternatively, they often serve as a go-between for grain traders to resale their allotment to the latter for a small profit of 10 to 20 birr that they may use to buy food or other basic items.

A common alteration that many households make is to stop or reduce purchasing *teff* to buy small amounts of baked *injera* from the neighborhood on a daily or mealtime basis. This allows them to avoid relatively large outlays and to acquire their food as they earn money on a daily basis.

Households also reduced purchases of food items other than cereals in response to food inflation and diminishing incomes. They were likely to reduce their purchases of *shiro*, making the smaller amounts last longer. Supplements or alternatives to the *shiro* such as split chickpeas or lentils were also likely to have the same fate. Frequently, households also reduced or eliminated vegetables such as kale, lettuce, onions, green pepper or potatoes to allocate their remaining cash towards the purchase of cereals and *shiro*. Other ingredients of the *shiro* or stews - oil, *berbere* or garlic - are reduced from households' grocery list from already small amounts as well.

Among the first food items that were eliminated as food prices began to climb were relatively costly food items such as pasta, meat, fruits, eggs and milk, which are bought mainly for children. Households are also likely to have severely curtailed their expenditures on clothes and entertainment early on.

As indicated above, a significant change in households' engagement with the market is the shift from occasional purchases of larger portions of items such as oil, kerosene, charcoal, sugar and coffee to daily purchases of miniscule amounts from *chercharo* or petty traders.

Regulation of food consumption

The reductions in food purchases described above force households to undertake cutbacks in food consumption in their attempts to make available food supplies last longer. Reductions in the amount of *injera* consumed is one of the most common types of rationing. This would mean that family members do not eat till they are full and their individual consumption declines to as low as half an *injera*. Ways of bringing about such reductions may involve allocation of individual portions of food. Commonly, cutbacks in food consumption only affect adults and older children while younger children may be spared from them. The elderly wife of the vegetable supplier, with a family size of 13, explained:

> I am the same if I eat or not. Children are the ones who have to eat and drink. It is not a problem if adults like us do not eat because we are more concerned about our children. We want our children to eat and drink and not be hungry. Their father comes in from a day of hard work and only thinks about the children. He does not think about food for himself. [*Kebele 09/10*]

Preceding or alongside such reductions in consumption of *injera,* households may mix teff flour with flour from cheaper cereals to bake and consume *injera* which has a somewhat different flavor and texture. Cereals such as wheat, maize, rice and sorghum can be mixed with or without teff for this purpose. A practice that has been widely adopted among food insecure households is to use maize as *leaven* with teff flour at a ratio of 5:20 for instance.

Another way of cutting down on food consumption is to replace *injera* with wheat bread which may be eaten with *shiro* or other condiments. Alternatively, families may make a meal of *qollo* or *nifro* which are roasted and boiled cereals or pulses. The contract cook in *kebele* 09/10 said:

> After working for a number of days on a cooking contract, I am able to buy legumes such as chickpeas. We boil these and eat them with some salt. There are times in the rainy season we do not eat *injera*. Even if it is costly, we buy fresh corn and eat it roasted. We then drink some water and go to bed. I do this frequently. We don't lack legumes. Otherwise, my 25 kilos of *teff* and 5 kilos of maize cannot last a whole month.

Other food types that can replace the more substantial *injera* or bread are *atmit* – a type of gruel made from cereals, or *beso*. On the other hand, costly foods such as pasta, rice and meat can be avoided to rely exclusively on *injera* and *shiro* instead. Foods meant for children such as eggs and milk can be eliminated as well.

Food rationing mechanisms also include reducing or altering the *shiro* that is the normal complement to *injera*. Ordinarily made from pulses such as peas or chickpeas, a recent practice is to mix in the cheaper vetch with peas. *Shiro* may also be made without oil, onions or *berbere* when these items or cash are in short supply, which results in a watery or less tasty product. The rare use of soya beans as a stew instead of *shiro* was also documented in the tailor's family.

When households are especially short of resources, they may eliminate *shiro* or any other stew from a meal as well. Such a meal is considered quiet sparse. Poor families may therefore eat *injera* or bread simply with green pepper, *berbere, mitmita,* salt or *sils,* a type of sauce made from tomatoes, *berbere* and salt.

Skipping meals

A common way of coping with food shortages in poor households is to skip one or more of the three meals of the day. Most often, family members do without one of the meals of the day, usually breakfast but sometimes lunch or dinner. Asked about how his family coped with high food prices in the past year which led to diminished food supplies, a young daily laborer in *kebele* 05/08 said, 'It is by doing without breakfast and the snack as a result of the food shortage. It was necessary to deprive ourselves. Our stomachs are now used to it.'

In times when household food deficits are especially severe, family members may skip up to 2 meals of the day. This often means that they only have lunch and leave out breakfast and dinner. Adults are more likely to skip meals. The 54-year old daily laborer in *kebele* 09/10 explained:

> I have to avoid dinner so that the children will eat. If they need to eat their lunch, I may have to do without it. I give them priority when household food stocks are low. When there is some food for dinner, they may have more of it while I have a bit of food before going to bed.

Other food strategies

Households also adjust their cooking practices in response to diminishing resources. A common practice is to cook *shiro* or another type of stew only once a day in order to save on onions, oil and fuel. This may be eaten for the three meals of the day, sometimes by warming it while adding *shiro*, salt and water to it.

The use of a children's food such as *faffa*, given to poor households as aid by NGOs, to feed the whole family is another desperate mechanism of dealing with food shortages. Several households included in this study were found to depend on this food for an extended period.

Some members of the family eat some or all of their meals outside the home as a way of reducing the demands on household food stocks. Young males who engage in various sorts of daily wage labor are especially likely to have their meals outside on a regular basis. In *Kebele 05/08*, many residents, including couples, were found to be eating at a community café run by a women's group for 3 birr per meal.

Income generating activities

Efforts to generate income are an important means of coping with food insecurity for poor urban households. Such households earn small amounts of income from a variety of activities that they have undertaken either on a long term basis or in response to the recent food crises. Either way, most of these activities only allow them to maintain the bare minimum subsistence levels.

The women who were involved in the study have been engaging in activities such as petty trading in vegetable and coal, collection of *chat* branches and waste paper for sale, cloth washing, baking *injera,* hair dressing, *arake* (liquor) sales, running a kiosk, begging and sending their daughter to the Middle East for domestic labor. The men in the study have been engaged in paid employment, casual labor, skilled work as a tailor, carpenter and carpenter's assistant, house rental and begging.

Many households depend on several income earners, including parents, children and others, in order to make ends meet. A single income earner is no longer sufficient to meet their subsistence needs. Frequently, male children would engage in work which would allow them to take care of most of their own needs and to sometimes give a bit of money to their families. In a household headed by a pensioner for instance, two teenagers worked as a daily laborer and maid mostly temporarily, and occasionally contributed bread to the family. In many households, children also were involved in income earning activities such as the production and sale of paper bags, which often interfered with their school attendance or studies.

Asset sales

Sales of assets in the form of household possessions can be a means of withstanding food and income shortfalls, albeit only temporarily. However, most respondents interviewed on this issue denied that they had ever engaged in asset sales, mainly because they had no assets to sell. One of the exceptions was a 42-year old woman who engaged in processing food for other households and who said, 'When I became sick in November and December last year and could not work, I sold my jewelry and bought some grain with it. I feel sad about selling them for the sake of my stomach'. Another 65-year old man who survived as a beggar had sold household furniture over the past 6 years, including wooden closet, a sofa set and kitchen utensils, for the purpose of buying food and paying off arrears in his rent.

<u>Social mechanisms</u>

Social networks can be an important source of protection against food insecurity for poor urban households. In the study communities, a few households were able to borrow money from relatives and acquaintances when they fell short of food. These included a daily laborer who was able to borrow as much as 300 birr when work opportunities in the telecom sector fell off in the rainy season; the 50-year old government worker who borrowed some money at the end of the month to make ends meet; and the 48-year old temporary domestic worker who borrowed small amounts of money to meet daily expenses. Others were able to borrow items such as *injera* and vegetables from petty traders, a form of loan called *dube*.

Quite a few respondents, however, said that they do not borrow food or money either because there was no one to borrow from or because they would not be able to repay the loan. Relatives generally could not be relied upon for such a purpose. Nevertheless, the 78-year old pensioner said that he was regularly able to request assistance in the form of money from acquaintances who were non-relatives. While it is possible to take a loan from an employing agency or from the micro-finance arm of the *kebele* administration, people were also often reluctant to make use of such sources because of their inability to repay the loan or generate income from it.

Other social networks and institutions in the neighborhoods offered a means of mutual support. Neighbors sometimes maintain rotating credit associations called *equb* or share meat or meals during holidays. Some funeral associations or *idirs* give out from 100 to 500 birr to all members or the poorer ones on holidays. Destitute or elderly members of the community are also given food during the holidays as well. However, such forms of support, including *equbs,* the distribution of money by *idirs* and sharing of meals during holidays appear to have declined markedly in these days of economic hardship and generalized food insecurity.

Reliance on aid

Several households involved in the study regularly received the high energy child feed, *faffa,* from NGOs but used it to feed the whole family because they regularly run short of food. The families of a factory worker, government worker and vegetable supplier reported maintaining this practice. These families used *faffa* to make porridge, gruel or a flat bread. Some families also received assistance in the form of wheat. Notably, the 30 year old employee of the local administration said that his family refused to accept any form of aid despite the lifelong difficult circumstances that they faced, saying, 'I never liked [receiving aid], because we always believed that that we should improve ourselves based on our own efforts. We did not accept assistance even in the past when we did not have anything' [*Kebele* 09/10].

Constraints on coping mechanisms

Poor households face a number of constraints in their efforts to cope with or overcome food insecurity. Illness, physical incapacity and old age were some of the more common constraints on the utilization and efficacy of these coping mechanisms. This was exemplified in the case of two elderly women prevented from direct involvement in *injera* baking due to a cancer or old age and a weak eye, consigning one of them to begging; illness arising from excessive exposure to the sun and nasal problems preventing a young girl from engaging in petty trading and hairdressing; physical weakness and pain in the hands constraining a woman's engagement in cloth washing; and eye problems and weakness in his legs preventing a pensioner from working as a guard.

Market constraints are another challenge facing individuals involved in some sort of income generating activity. Weaknesses in the market in the form of high prices which constrained supplies of *arake* (liquor) confronted the wife of a daily laborer who wanted to engage in trading it; diminishing resources overall which weakened the demand for cloth washing services of an elderly woman; excessive competition which adversely affected the involvement of a petty trader's teenage sons in the resale of tin cans; and the low profits of petty trading in vegetables realized by the wife of the manager of a community café.

The lack of capital is also a constraint on people's efforts to engage in various income earning activities such as trading, a food business and shoe production. Many of them failed to gain credit from funds made available by the *kebele* due to the need for a guarantor and their fear of being unable to repay. A woman was unable to join a savings and credit association which was just being established due to her full time engagement in daily wage labor.

Households' coping mechanisms in the form of self-employment initiatives can also be weakened by certain government policies and actions. The harassment of women for engaging in petty trading on the streets and the high rents imposed on individuals who attempt to open mini-businesses from their home or other sites are examples of such outcomes.

4.9 Prospects and plans regarding food security

Participants in the study were also given the chance to discuss their perspectives regarding their prospects and plans with respect to the food security of their families. Quite a few of them, including the contract cook, the tailor's wife, daily laborer and manager of the community café, felt that their conditions would either not improve or would be worse in the future. Their assessment of current trends was the primary reason for their pessimism. Other reasons such as the adverse impact of population growth and the prospect of displacement due to a housing development project facing most residents of *kebele* 07/14 were cited as other reasons. For example, the tailor's wife said, "I myself have given up hope. I don't think anything better will come. It has become dark. I don't think anyone will be able to live a good life or be happy" [*Kebele* 07/14].

A large number of respondents, on the other hand, believed that their food security and life conditions would improve in the future. This group based their optimism on the economic development they saw occurring; their hope that prices would stabilize or that they would get a job; and the availability of credit. Several of them hoped that their children would get jobs and support them. From the list of respondents, the more youthful ones were more likely to have a positive outlook regarding the future.

A good portion of respondents were also not able to plan to improve their food security. Several thought that their lack of money or a job did not put them in a position to plan for the future. It was the struggle to survive rather than the future that they were pre-occupied with. The prospect of displacement due to the housing project in *Kebele* 07/14 was too stressful to allow a pensioner in that *kebele* to plan for the future. Another woman chose to put her faith in God rather than preparing plans of her own.

However, even more respondents said they were taking or planning to take steps to improve their food security. Several had been applying for various jobs or a loan. A couple of them were undergoing training in order to improve their livelihood. Others said that they were educating their children who they hoped would help them attain a better life. A few women wanted to join or had joined a women's credit and saving association. A young mother was interested in opening a laundry business if she could get like-minded co-borrowers for a loan from the *kebele*, while the daughter of the elderly local government worker wanted to go to the Middle East as a domestic worker. She said:

> Life is difficult. My family is poor and I now have a baby. I cannot think of supporting them while I am living in this country. Therefore, I am planning to go to a foreign place and help my family attain a better life, God willing! [*Kebele 05/08*]

4.10 Perspectives regarding actions that would improve food security

Communities which have to deal with food insecurity can be expected to have special insights regarding ways of alleviating it. Participants in the study were therefore given the opportunity to offer their opinions regarding actions that government and non-government agencies should take to improve their food security. Their recommendations were related to the supply and access to food, employment or incomes, and production of food.

There was a widely accepted view among respondents that the free market was responsible for the steady rise in food prices and that the government should therefore strengthen control over food prices. This included calls for controlling the market by monitoring and regulating grain traders. One of the daughters of the elderly local government worker in *Kebele* 05/08 explained:

> The government should investigate greedy grain traders who are involved in illegal trading in order to accumulate their own capital and bring them before the law. This is because we cannot survive if they are not eliminated. Also, the problem comes mainly from the free market, which is unnecessary because it is hurting the country.... The illegal trade in grain has to stop.

A related notion that appeared to be commonly held regardless of its correspondence to reality is that the export of cereals, especially *teff*, was responsible for rising prices. A few respondents therefore felt that the cereal exports they believed existed should be terminated.

As another way of addressing high food prices, a number of respondents recommended that the consumer associations which are now operating, albeit quiet ineffectively, should be strengthened. Suggestions regarding how to do this included providing them with adequate space to operate in, access to credit, financial control mechanisms and access to adequate grain supplies at an affordable price. Others suggested the revival of the old cooperative shops which would make basic commodities available to residents in an affordable manner.

The other category of recommendations was concerned with enhancing employment opportunities which would improve food security among beneficiaries. Skill training in various areas was seen as one of the ways of achieving this. The selection and design of such training based on a proper assessment of market demands was recommended as well. In addition, respondents suggested organizing people for training and cooperative enterprises, and giving them work space as well. Furthermore, the expansion of industries, implementation of work projects and a positive approach to employment creation and protection were emphasized by others. A couple of study participants mentioned raising salaries and pensions.

A final set of recommendations addressed the promotion of food production. To achieve this, efforts to enhance farmer productivity and to encourage people to enter the agricultural sector were recommended.

5. Conclusion

In the last several years but especially since the beginning of 2008, food consumption in poor households has declined to the bare minimum. This was manifested in very low amounts, variety and quality of food they consumed and the need to skip one to two of the three meals of the day. Although small children are often protected from such dietary shortfalls, they may be exposed to inadequate diets as well. Women seem more likely to cut their dietary intake in favor of other family members.

The unprecedented rise in food prices accounted for much of the decline in food intake. For many households, however, multiple factors including high food prices combined to bring about reductions in their food consumption. Such factors included losses of jobs or income sources, poverty, unemployment, contraction of market demands for people's goods and services, and the decision to invest in job training.

Chronic hunger was a common outcome of the cutbacks in food consumption. While some appeared to have adapted to dietary inadequacy, others experienced physical weakness, emotional distress and hopelessness. Similarly, the occurrence of weight loss, illness and declines in educational and work performance in families exposed to food shortages was variable.

The study has also identified the characteristics of the various mechanisms that households use to cope with food insecurity. Food-based coping mechanisms involve reductions in food purchases and dietary portions; altering or eliminating food types and ingredients; relying on cheaper and less desirable food types and varieties; and skipping meals. Income generating activities tended to yield diminishing or fluctuating incomes that were earned from multiple sources or by different individuals. Asset sales were not possible for most urban households who lacked significant disposable assets. Social mechanisms that are sometimes a source of help for households confronted with food or cash shortages such as loans, rotating credit groups, burial associations and food aid are not able to provide much support currently.

Variable levels of optimism and ability to take steps with respect to improving their food security were observable among community members. Their views regarding actions that could be taken by governmental and non-governmental bodies were concerned with strengthened control over food prices and the grain exports that they believed existed, and strengthening consumers' cooperative societies, employment opportunities and food production.

6. Policy and Programme Recommendations

As shown in the study, poor households in Addis Ababa and probably in other urban centers are facing a quiet desperate situation with respect to their food security. There is therefore a need for urgent adoption of standard and innovative policy and programmatic initiatives to address urban food insecurity.

6.1 Developing an urban food security strategy

The food security strategies adopted by the country so far have focused on rural areas. However, the study has indicated that the food insecurity level among poor urban households is comparable to conditions among vulnerable rural households. It is therefore critical to include an urban food security strategy in subsequent poverty reduction strategies in order to protect the urban poor from food insecurity. Such a step can include the following food security-oriented initiatives.

6.2 Initiating an urban safety net programme

The mainly rural-based safety net programme should be expanded to cover the most vulnerable urban households whose incomes do not allow them to meet their food needs. Such a safety net programme would consist of food or cash transfers which may be targeted on the basis of occupation or income (Dorosh 2009; Anderson 1987). These transfers can involve public works related to sanitary activities, improvement of urban infrastructure and landscape, or community service. They would also include direct support to the labor-poor such as the elderly and people living with HIV/AIDS, and food supplements for children, including orphans and vulnerable children.

6.3 Improving the grain subsidy programme

The sale of government subsidized imported wheat through ration shops has contributed to the stabilization of cereal prices and enhanced household access to food. Nevertheless, its inability to reduce cereal prices rapidly and to avail subsidized wheat regularly at the local level, its limitation to one type of cereal, the imposition of a minimum quota and the lack of targeting has weakened its impact on poor households.

One of the ways of strengthening the programme is to improve the operation of the ration shops by taking steps to ensure the regular availability of subsidized grain and eliminating minimum quotas. The introduction of mechanisms to target poor households for grain sales can be another way of maximizing the benefits to them. The redirection of the subsidies from imported wheat to domestic cereals can also better meet the preferences of households if ways can be found to prevent this from bringing about further rises in cereal prices. The selection of less-preferred cereals such as black teff or maize for subsidization can utilize self-targeting to benefit poorer consumers.

An alternative option is to release subsidized cereals through market channels instead of government-run ration shops, which may be a more effective way of regulating market prices of cereals. This option also takes advantage of the strengths of the market in availing demand-driven quantities and types of grain to purchasers.

A food stamp programme is yet another means of subsidizing food to poor consumers who can buy food stamps from the government at reduced prices to buy quantities of cereals at higher value from the market. This option eliminates the need to establish government sales outlets.

6.4 Strengthening consumers' cooperatives

Consumers' Cooperatives lack the financial resources, market networks and storage space to provide more affordable and diversified cereals to consumers. They need further support in meeting these shortfalls.

6.5 Employment Creation

The lack of employment or low incomes are obviously integral to urban food insecurity. The steps suggested below are aimed at augmenting the various employment creating or promoting programmes currently being implemented in urban centers.

    i. Strengthen support for the small and micro enterprises programme:

        a. Strengthen small and micro enterprises by addressing financial and space-related constraints facing them;

        b. Strengthen current initiatives to review collateral requirements of savings and credit agencies and to construct multi-storied buildings for enterprises;

        c. Give special attention to food processing enterprises which will strengthen women's income and enhance access to food for the poor.

    ii. Strengthen employment skills and opportunities:

        a. Substantially expand skill training for out of school youth and adults;

        b. Introduce innovative schemes to afford credit to individuals;

        c. Strengthen the recently initiated programme to link job-seekers and domestic or overseas employers.

    iii. Adopt an employment-friendly policy and regulatory environment:

a. Review rent and taxation requirements on small and micro businesses;

b. Provide working space for enterprises that have been displaced by road building or other projects;

c. Reduce the harassment of street vendors and set aside areas in favorable business sections for them.

6.6 Supporting commercial and urban food production and processing

In addition to efforts to enhance access to food and income, it is necessary to pursue opportunities for food production and more diversified options for food processing and use such as the following:

i. Significantly expand commercial food production on medium-sized and large farms in the lowland areas of the country.

ii. Promote urban agriculture by supporting production of early maturing crops, root crops and small ruminants and by temporarily availing unused open spaces for this purpose (Dessalegn Rahmato, personal communication). The latter will require a review of the policy, legal and regulatory framework governing the use of land that has not been brought into use either before or after being allocated for investment or residential purposes;

iii. Support the development of locally processed nutritious foods which meet the needs of households in terms of price, quantity and taste. This would include marketable street foods, which are used widely in other parts of Africa.

6.7 Addressing child nutrition

It would also be important to take additional steps to directly address the nutrition of children.

i. Give sufficient attention to improved child nutrition practices in the recently adopted Urban Health Extension Programme. The strengthened promotion of family planning in this programme will also allow households to take better care of fewer children.

ii. Introduce school feeding which will have a strong impact on child nutrition and school attendance and performance.

References

Anderson, Pinstrup. 1987. Food Prices and the poor in developing countries. In *Food policy: Integrating supply, distribution and consumption*, edited by J. Price Gittinger, Joanne Leslie and Caroline Hoisington. The Johns Hopkins University Press.

Central Statistical Authority. 2005. Report on the 2004/5 Household Income, Consumption & Expenditure Survey, Addis Ababa.

Dorosh, P.A. 2009. Price stabilization, international trade and national cereal stocks: World Price shocks and policy response in South Asia. *Food Security,* Vol. 1, No. 2 (June): 137 -149.

Emebet Mulugeta. 2008. Negotiating poverty: Problems and coping strategies of women in five cities of Ethiopia. In *Urban poverty in Ethiopia: The economic and social adaptations of women,* edited by Emebet Mulugeta. Addis Ababa: Addis Ababa University Press.

Maxwel, D., C. Levin, M. Armar-Kelmesu, M. Ruel, S. Morris, C. Ahiadelle. 2000. Urban livelihoods and food and nutrition security in Greater Accra. Research Report 112, April. International Food Policy Research Institute.

Ministry of Finance and Economic Development (MoFED). 2008. Dynamics of growth and poverty in Ethiopia (1995/96-2004/05). Development Planning and Research Department (DPRD). Ministry of Finance and Economic Development (MOFED), Addis Ababa.

Netsanet Teklehaymanot. 2008. *Dynamics of poverty in Addis Ababa: The case of Arada, Addis Ketema and Lideta Sub-cities.* FSS Research Report, No. 3. Addis Ababa: Forum for Social Studies.

Ruel, M.T., and J. L. Garett. 2004. Features of urban food and nutrition security and considerations for successful urban programming. *Electronic Journal of Agricultural Development Economics* 1, no. 2: 242-271. FAO, Agricultural and Development Economics Division.

von Braun, J. 2008. *High food prices: The what, who and how of proposed policy actions.* Policy Brief, May. International Food Policy Research Institute.

World Bank. 1998. Participatory poverty assessment of Ethiopia. World Bank Discussion Paper.

Annex 1

Socio-Economic Characteristics of IDI Participants

Employment type	Sex	Age	Marital status	Family size	Income/ month
1. Coal sales	F	55	Divorced	6	3-5 br/day
2. Begging & cloth washing	F	65	Widow	3	-
3. *Injera* baking & *berbere* prep	F	42	Married	7	-
4. Daily laborer	M	28	Married	3	500
5. Nanny/cleaner – KG/NGO	F	28	Married	6	250
6. *Injera* baking & sales	F	50	Married	7	-
7. Cleaner & messenger – GO	F	23	Single	8	375
8. Sanitation – GO	M	55	Married	10	516
9. Housewife/ Husband - private sector	F	24	Married	5	500
10. Guard/carpenter	M	67	Widower	5	472
11. Unemployed/ Husband vegetable supplier	F	50	Married	13	200
12. Begging	M	65	Married	3	-
13. Contract Cook	F	36	Divorced	4	250
14. Small trade	F	51	Married	4	4-5 br/day
15. Pensioner	M	60	Married	7	450
16. Auditor - GO	M	32	Single	12	900
17. Daily laborer	F	38	Widow	5	300
18. Daily laborer	M	54	Married	7	15 br/day
19. Legal officer- GO	M	30	Single	8	700
20. Unemployed/house rental	F	60	Widow	6	400
21. Petty trade	F	47	Divorced	6	150
22. Domestic work	F	48	Married	6	-
23. Carpenter's assistant	M	38	Married	5	300
24. Tailor	M	72	Married	6	250
25. Daily laborer/house rental	M	44	Married	6	200
26. Factory worker	F	19	Married	4	300
27. Small machine producer	M	22	Single	3	500
28. Manager - public cafe	M	40	Married	4	400
29. Pensioner	M	78	Married	7	190

Annex 2

Glossary of Amharic Terms

Ambasha	A type of wheat bread usually made as a round pie
Arake	A local liquor distilled from fermented cereals
Atmit	A gruel made from cereal flour
Berbere	Processed red pepper widely used to prepare stew
Berd	A widely recognized illness arising from exposure to cold air
Chercharo	Sales of basic commodities conducted by petty traders
Dube	Informal credit in the form of cash or in-kind offered to households by shopkeepers or traders
Enset	The false banana plant
Equb	The widely prevalent informal rotating credit groups
Faffa	A high energy child food commercially produced for children
Idir	Funeral association that is widely prevalent in Ethiopia
Injera	The thin flat bread which is made from *teff* and/or other cereals
Kebele	The smallest unit of local government
Mitch	An illness widely believed to arise from exposure to environmental conditions and causing fever, cramps or skin sores
Mitmita	A hot condiment made from various spices
Nifro	Food consisting of boiled cereals or pulses
Qinche	A food made from boiled split wheat cooked with oil or butter
Qita	A thin flat bread

Qocho	A type of bread made from the root of the false banana plant
Qollo	A snack food consisting of roasted cereals and pulses
Shiro	A stew which is made from pea flour cooked with oil and onions
Sils	A paste made from tomatoes and processed red pepper